SELECTED POEMS

CHRISTOPHER REID

Selected Poems ～

faber and faber

First published in 2011
by Faber and Faber Ltd
Bloomsbury House
74–77 Great Russell Street
London WC1B 3DA

Typeset by CB editions, London
Printed in England by T. J. International Ltd, Padstow, Cornwall

A CIP record for this book
is available from the British Library

ISBN 978–0–571–27327–0

10 9 8 7 6 5 4 3 2 1

Contents

Arcadia

In this crayoned dream-town,
the chimneys think smoke
and every house is lovingly
Battenburged with windows.

A studious invention:
these strange, ecstatic folk,
who tower above their dwellings
and whose trees are deckled biscuits,

nuggeted with fruit.
As they step among the traffic
that lurches down the road
on its long sum of noughts,

they look like damaged packages,
targets for pin limbs,
and yet they contrive to greet us
with smiles like black bananas.

A Whole School of Bourgeois Primitives

Our lawn in stripes, the cat's pyjamas,
rain on a sultry afternoon

and the drenching, mnemonic smell this brings us
surging out of the heart of the garden:

these are the sacraments and luxuries
we could not do without.

Welcome to our peaceable kingdom,
where baby lies down with the tiger rug

and bumblebees roll over like puppies
inside foxglove bells . . .

Here is a sofa, hung by chains
from a gaudy awning.

Two puddles take the sun
in ribbon-patterned canvas chairs.

Our television buzzes like a fancy tie,
before the picture appears –

and jockeys in Art Deco caps and blouses
caress their anxious horses,

looking as smart as the jacks on playing-cards
and as clever as circus monkeys.

Douanier Rousseau had no need to travel
to paint the jungles of his paradise.

One of his tigers, frightened by a thunder-storm,
waves a tail like a loose dressing-gown cord:

it does not seem to match the coat quite,
but is ringed and might prove dangerous.

A Valve against Fornication

Biblical families begat, begat . . .
Aunt So-and-so, sprigged-out in a prodigal hat,
swoops on the birdie with her eagle eye –
poor, blurred Aunt Sally, one
(and but one) of a claque of maudlin
country-churchyard hens.

Now time has trumped another resurrection
out of this ample ground, where guests
of a wedding wander the graveyard.
We are like broad
sunflowers of empty circumspection,
touched and turned by the everlasting sun.

Deucalion flung this rubble
down on the grass: family headstones,
rolls of the gentry dead.
We pat them on the back, as if they were dogs;
or crouch to read such recondite catalogues:
names in a babel of chiselling, cryptic
runes of the weather, blotting-paper script.

Here is our vicar in his laundered smock,
trying to shake the hands of all his
rambling flock, while Bo-Peep
bridesmaids totter round his feet.
We are the famous human Venn diagram, where
two family circles coincide
in bridegroom and bride.
Bells go mad, living so near to heaven.
Speaking with tongues, they summon and send us away.

Canapés and circuses, of course!
                              But why
have all these gentlemen come
wearing the same disguise, with every
waistcoat-W unbuttoned so,
every top-hat fished from a velvet drum?
Waiters juggle by with trays.
Give me a plate of cataleptic
shrimps on thumbs of buttered bread!

A Holiday from Strict Reality

Here we are at the bay
of intoxicating discoveries,
where mathematicians
in bathing-trunks and bikinis
sit behind the wheels
of frisky little speedboats
and try out new angles
to the given water.

Everything that we see
in this gilded paradise
is ours to make use of:
palm-trees on the marine drive,
nature's swizzlesticks,
stir the afternoon air
to a sky-blue cocktail
of ozone and dead fish.

All day long
the punctilious white yachts
place their set-squares
against our horizon,
as we lie around on mats
and soak up the heat,
cultivating a sun-peel
that grows like lichen.

A restless volleyball
skips between four figures
like a decimal point,
but the ornamental beach bum,
who lives under an old boat,
picks at his guitar
and contemplates the plangent
hollow of its navel.

In the hotel bar,
alcoholic maraccas
and, on a high glass balcony,
a pompous royal family
of apéritif bottles...
Ernesto the barman
tots up a long bill,
castanetting with his tongue.

Utopian Farming

'Every nation is to be considered advisedly, and not to provoke
them by any disdain, laughing, contempt or suchlike, but to
use them with prudent circumspection, with all gentleness, and
courtesy.'
Sebastian Cabot, *Ordinances* . . .

Great maps of dung obliterate the path –
Elizabethan guesswork, or
the aftermath of Ayrshire cows,
come to give milk in the morning.

Real life resumes as we follow them,
browsing with brooms,
to smudge away these new-found continents,
suds of urinous seas.

Our delicate tubs of fecundity
never quite know which way to go,
hung between legs with swashbuckling,
cream-bag udders, in lieu of rudders.

With kohl-eyed figureheads, beautiful
and dim – if they prance
out of line (manoeuvring sideways),
we morris-dance them back as we can.

Meanwhile, the pigs comport
themselves in their sties like Falstaffian
generals, slumped
with buckled muzzles and small, pouched eyes.

We are like sutlers, bringing them water and nuts,
or leaning down to tickle their flanks,
white bristles stiff, as if
from years of soldierly grooming.

Our service seems a kind of a meditation,
and meditation akin to ridicule.
I love to be here, private,
subversive and free, in friendly company,

where pigs on tip-toes
piss with such a haunted look,
you'd swear there was something amiss,
and sleepwalking cattle dump wherever they go.

Hens are galleon-hulled: we take them by storm,
plucking the eggs from under their bodies,
bony and warm – freebooters against
a proud and panicky-wheeling armada.

Baldanders

Pity the poor weightlifter
alone on his catasta,

who carries his pregnant belly
in the hammock of his leotard

like a melon wedged in a shopping-bag...
A volatile prima donna,

he flaps his fingernails dry,
then – squat as an armchair –

gropes about the floor
for inspiration, and finds it there.

His Japanese muscularity
resolves to domestic parody.

Glazed, like a mantelpiece frog,
he strains to become

the World Champion (somebody, answer it!)
Human Telephone.

H. Vernon

The butcher, tired of his bloody work,
has made a metaphysical joke.

Five pigs' heads on a marble counter
leer lopsidedly out of the window

and scare away the passers-by.
The vision is far too heavenly.

With ears like wings, these pallid putti –
hideous symbols of eternal beauty –

relax on parsley and smirk about
their newly-disembodied state.

A van draws up outside. The butcher
opens his glass door like St Peter,

as angels heave in flanks of pork
that are strung with ribs like enormous harps.

Our Commune

'A jungle is a machine for climbing,'
somebody said,
and then set up this aluminium plumbing

to prove it. Pipes intersect neatly
overhead,
where most of us lounge and dangle, or sprout directly

out of bare concrete, with angular U-
bends instead
of branches. Very Bauhaus! We make do

with just enough room to swing a monkey,
go to bed
on shelves and indulge in public hanky-panky

like the true Cynics. It could be ideal,
but is it? Dead
bored, a pink-tongued gorilla picks a meal

out of his armpit, reclining as if
at a Roman spread;
his right hand mimes the cigarette that would give him

perfect pleasure. Spider monkeys,
who nurse a dread
of stopping still, play tag on their trapeze

and ignore the puny macaque that hangs
like an old, underfed,
market chicken from one of the exercise-rings.

We study bananas and meditation.
That foul shed
over there houses our guru, the wryly patient

mandrill, whose yellow satyr's beard,
fangs, bright-red
nose and fluted cheeks make him so revered.

Auburn, olive, ashy, white:
every thread
of his coat is remarkable. His hands are folded tight

across his apron, but offer him
a hunk of bread
and he'll show you his eloquent brown-and-lilac bottom.

Our Host Speaks

Fog can cancel most things.
The water corrodes.
We are lucky still to be here
in this temporary city,
where windows are defended
by filigrees of dwindling rust,
and minor marine gods bleach and eat
the barn-doors of palazzi.

The old stone blots and softens.
Our citizens promenade
like ghosts apprehended through drizzling twilight
on marble veined and stained
by ancient seepings. This tessera crumbles
like a block of cork,
while others are vellum, buff, steak-red
or spattered like quails' eggs.

We delight not just in surfaces,
but in their relinquishment as well.
Walls flake like bark.
Rope grows a waterlogged mane
and lions modify
their evangelical features.
You can grey your fingers
on the dust of endless eponymous saints.

The priests make an oriental sound,
droning, gonging the echoes off
celestial domes in mordant pleasure.
Churches dock
close to the pink and ochre squares
where pigeons gather
like applicants for the post of Holy Spirit,
or a drowned Christ hangs out to dry.

You must let me show you
the tiny boudoir-church
that is my favourite,
with its touch-worn Ovidian altar-frieze.
Here, satyrs, popping pods, bull-tritons, leaves,
the innocent raptures of sexy mermaids,
flourish from marble. And Heaven itself
is graced by an off-centre patch of damp.

Three Sacred Places in Japan

Practical Zen

Hush. Timber-smells. The grain and sheen
of floorboards buffed by unshod feet.
A dim chamber, with its paper screen
and brisk ink-daubs, where the abbot sat . . .

This small pavilion affords
a full view of two cosmic gardens:
here, gravel combed like a placid sea
and set with islands of rude stone;

there, undulant moss as terra firma.
I thought that I was quite alone,
until I saw the apparition –

a monk with meditative murmur
bowing his bristle-stippled head,
to cull weeds from their dusty bed.

A Complex Sentence from the Envoy's Memoirs

I met the obscure god
of their trumpery summerhouses
in a dank shed by the lake
with its mad square-dance of midges,

where dragonflies, stunned and coupling,
hovered above dead pads
and torpid, subaqueous fronds,
and I looked into his bronze,

bucket-smooth face to find
some sacrament of the mind
that transcended all clutter and swelter,

but nothing gave, and I left him,
smugly beatitudinous,
alone on his artichoke throne.

Itsukushima

On guard against the harbour fish,
a dozen anglers line the quay.
Rowboats, a few feet out to sea,
moored empty, shrug their bafflement.

Big barrel-drums, salt-seasoned wood,
furnish apartments of the shrine
that's built on stout piles like a pier.
I see the point of worshipping here.

Below, the tiny, tender crabs
tango in shallows, risking land,
then dashing to sockets of sludged sand.

Green seaweed wraiths, a beer can, drunk,
are tugged by the tide . . .
                 You Nothings, bless
me in my next-to-nothingness!

The Ambassador

Life in this narrow neck
of the galaxy reads like a rebus –
one damned, inscrutable
poser after another.
The planet surface is cluttered
with objects: wherever my feet fall,
something gives like a gibus
or jumps away with a squeak.

Impossible to tell,
as it were, between living and dead.
An innocent-looking box
will suddenly burst one side
with garish laughter. From hiding
behind a babel of bricks,
a three-inch ladybird
creeps out on stridulant wheels.

Most of the populace
turn out to be ciphers, dummies,
mere animalcules of stuffing
and stitching. I talk to them
politely, but they, it would seem,
are determined to say nothing
(although, if you press their tummies,
some do make a querulous noise).

And so I follow a nervous,
diplomatic course:
keeping my counsel; listening;
attending rigid tea parties
with mad-eyed, plastic beauties
and blotto frogs; whispering
and peering in through the front door
of the tiny, bourgeois palace.

If I lose my patience,
forgive me. Yesterday,
I kicked a troop of saluting
soldiers down the stairs;
but at heart I still adhere
to the maxim that, through a studious
reading of chaos, we may
arrive at the grammar of civilisation.

Bathos

Yes, I had come to the right place: the jumbo
cheeseplant languishing at a window told me,
and the lift's bisecting doors confirmed it.

Emboxment and apotheosis followed
at once. I approved the fragrance of a late
cigar, while numbers counted themselves discreetly.

Time to remember the whole of my wasted life:
evenings of apathy; vague, extravagant walks;
the cat bemused by my keyboard melancholias.

And now this feeling, as if I had been deftly
gathered into an upward oubliette,
to arrive – where? – at a meadow of sulphurous carpet.

There was a young girl at her desk with three
telephones. I spoke to her politely. Magic!
I heard: 'Mr Dixon will be with you shortly.'

A huge vase full of plastic flowers stood
on a ledge, where an old man, passing, bent to savour them.
The unregenerate minutes turned and turned.

Of Mr Dixon's office, I can recall
the photograph of his wife, some freckled apples
and an alarming stuffed owl under its bell-jar.

But everything else has vanished. Stepping out
of the lift, beyond the ailing cheeseplant, I
looked back and wondered if something important was missing.

The Traveller

First, I plotted my course
by all the wrong clocks of London,
the constellation of friends
whose secrets I alone could read,
hoping by venture to navigate
a route to the heart of the dream.

But you know how every dream
is apt to follow its own course.
I saw the great buses navigate
the capes and inlets of London
and tried in their commerce to read
some entente between my friends –

the archipelago of friends
that spattered, in my dream,
a map too dazzling to read.
I was always miles off course,
trusting to currents in London
that only a fool would navigate.

The eldritch gulls, who navigate
with their far-flung friends
the rowdy sea-air above London,
complicated the dream.
They were not lost, of course
(with an open city to read),

but anyone else could read,
in their attempts to navigate
the diplomatic course
of conduct proper to friends,
a wild fear of the dream-
cartography of London.

Undaunted, I travelled through London
and, learning how to read
the prosy flow of the old dream,
I found that I could navigate
between clocks, buses, gulls, friends,
some kind of a course.

Dear friends, I had hoped in due course
to bring back my dream-map of London
for you to read and to navigate...

At the Wrong Door

A bank manager's rapid signature
of hair on the bath enamel, twist
and tail, to confirm that I have missed
you by a minute; mat on the floor,

stamped vigorously with wet; your
absence palpable in the misty,
trickling, inexorcisable ghost
that occupies the whole mirror –

I cannot rub it away – the room
clings to me with such a perfume
of soap and sweat, that I can only

stop to think how somewhere else
you may be standing, naked, lonely,
amid a downfall of dampish towels.

Pale-Blue Butterflies

Once again, magically
and without official notification,
it was the time of year
for the pale-blue butterflies to arrive.

They came in their millions –
an army composed entirely of stragglers
filling the sky,
the gust-driven trash of migration.

Working in the garden,
bent on our solicitous pillage
of the strawberry beds,
out of the corners of our eyes
we saw the first of them descend.

What were we to these multitudinous creatures?
A point of reference
on the transcontinental journey
from A to B?
Hardly even that.

For a week they came
lighting on our favoured blooms,
as detachable as earrings,
but so common
that nobody, except the wobbliest of toddlers,
bothered to try to catch them.

Yet it was not exactly
a mutual indifference.
I'm sure that I was not alone
in feeling, as I do each year,
that this would be the perfect time
to mend the whole of one's life.

Later, when the butterflies had gone,
we loaded our van with the last of the strawberries
and drove to town
to be given the official market price.

There followed an unscheduled
season of summer thunders:
colossal rearrangements
somewhere at the back of the mind.

A Tune

Stammered on a mandolin,
an old sentimental tune
from an open doorway in summer:
of course, it's only a radio thinking aloud
and nobody paying much attention.
Who can afford to lose tears over music these days?

I have heard the same song
in numerous clever disguises –
embellished with hesitations and surprise chords
by my cousin, the promising fiddler;
crooned almost silently by women in kitchens
to lull children or coax the rising of the dough.

And then there was the dance band
that came twice a year to our village.
My father explained the workings of the bass tuba,
how the breath was obliged to travel patiently
through those shiny intestines, before it could issue
in a sound halfway between serious and rude.

Its thoughtful flatulence underscored
both the quick dances, and the slow ones
where the men took the women in their proprietorial embrace
and moved about the floor with an ostentatious dreaminess.
The band played an arrangement of the very tune
that someone's radio is remembering right now.

I dare say it means something to you as well.
Amazing, how a piece of nonsense like this can survive,
more obstinate than any national anthem.
Perhaps they will dig it out again for my funeral:
a six-piece band ought to be sufficient,
with wind, an accordion, drums and at least one ceremonious
tuba.

Annals

Someone ought to write
the annals of the villages
on this bank of the river.
Conferences, statutes
and the economic forecasts
printed in the newspaper
are naturally important,
but there is much to learn, too,
from the sayings of old women
and the deaths of pigs.
I wish to propose
that a trustworthy historian
chosen by the Ministry of Culture
should spend some time among us.
He would meet my neighbour, the patriarch,
ninety years old,
who lies all day in bed
under a patchwork coverlet
which is really a symbolic map of Heaven,
but knows where every cucumber grows
and how much it will fetch
at the market in town.
His oldest son is a specialist
in the science of clouds
and never gets the weather wrong.
Of his seven children,
five of them female,
there is none without some deep knowledge:
of the different kinds of *eau de vie*,
of the magic language of cursing,

of money, flowers, childbed.
Beyond them lives the village mechanic,
a pious and reclusive man.
He attends all celebrations, however,
where music is required,
playing his violin faster and faster,
before wrapping it up again
in a square of black velvet
and returning home with it alone.
A boy in the village
is learning the Bible off by heart;
there are bets on when he will reach
the end of Deuteronomy.
The priest drinks too much,
but will give anyone who asks for it
his recipe against mosquito bites.
Last year two notable deaths occurred:
one woman was lifted by the wind
and deposited in the river,
where malevolent spirits dragged her to the bottom;
another choked, it is said,
on a fragment of fingernail.
Our landscape is enriched
by rumour and the discussion of prodigies.
Every day, history takes place,
even when nothing happens.
I believe these things should be written down
and published in the metropolis
as a matter of national pride.
An eminent scholar must be assigned the task:

not someone who scribbles little poems,
but a lucid stylist,
a practitioner of unambiguous prose.

The Oriental Gallery

Shadrach, Meshach and Abednego –
three pots from the same kiln.
Their Chinese maker must have been pleased
to see them emerge unscathed from the firing.

He was in the position of God.
They were his faithful servants, showing
by their unblemished complexions and perfect poise
how Nebuchadnezzar can be outsmarted.

Forgive me if I prefer the pieces
on other shelves: bottles with cricked
necks, and the jar that dribbles
its glaze like a sloppily fed baby.

Even more moving are the broken patterns
of pots that wanted to be earth again.

An Angel

An angel flew by
and the electricity dimmed.
It was like a soft jolt
to the whole of being.
I raised my eyes from the poems
that lay on the kitchen table,
the work of a friend, now dead.

It should not have mattered.
As the light glowed again,
I ought to have continued reading,
but that single pause
terrified me.
We say of the old
that they tremble on the brink.
I found that I was trembling.

Perhaps the black country nights
encourage superstition.
I remembered the angels
that had visited people I knew,
not hurrying past them
and merely stirring the air,
but descending with the all-inclusive
wingspan of annunciation
to obliterate them totally –
and I rose to my feet.

That one brief indecision
of the electric light
in a night of solitude
showed me how weak I was.
The poems on the table
lay where I had left them,
not knowing they had been abandoned.

Realism

I have an idea for a film.
It will begin with a birth:
not the conventional euphemisms,
but pictures of the real thing –
mucky and time-consuming
like some operation in charcuterie,
where the child is produced
with a great deal of awkward business
in its ugliest guise:
a little howling blood sausage.

At the end of the film
there will be a death
and this, too, will be shown
in every possible detail:
nothing omitted
from the final grotesque drama
of spasms and incontinence –
just the events as they occur.

And what, you may ask,
will happen in between?
I haven't decided yet,
but at least I can promise
years and years of realism –
what our people have always required,
but never yet been given.

What the Uneducated Old Woman Told Me

That she was glad to sit down.
That her legs hurt in spite of the medicine.
That times were bad.
That her husband had died nearly thirty years before.
That the war had changed things.
That the new priest looked like a schoolboy and you could
    barely hear him in church.
That pigs were better company, generally speaking, than
    goats.
That no one could fool her.
That both her sons had married stupid women.
That her son-in-law drove a truck.
That he had once delivered something to the President's
    palace.
That his flat was on the seventh floor and that it made her
    dizzy to think of it.
That he brought her presents from the black market.
That an alarm clock was of no use to her.
That she could no longer walk to town and back.
That all her friends were dead.
That I should be careful about mushrooms.
That ghosts never came to a house where a sprig of rosemary
    had been hung.
That the cinema was a ridiculous invention.
That the modern dances were no good.
That her husband had had a beautiful singing voice, until
    drink ruined it.
That the war had changed things.
That she had seen on a map where the war had been fought.
That Hitler was definitely in Hell right now.

That children were cheekier than ever.
That it was going to be a cold winter, you could tell from the
    height of the birds' nests.
That even salt was expensive these days.
That she had had a long life and was not afraid of dying.
That times were very bad.

A Box

Imagine a box, not a very big one,
but containing the following indispensable items:
a bed, a soup bowl, a landscape of mists and birches,
the words spoken by a pensive mother,
the absence of a father, several books including
a dictionary with a torn spine
and the works of the troubadours, a small photograph
in which the wince of a girl in sunlight is the main point,
a document with a stamp and a signature,
a message received from the friend of a friend,
a journey by train, an odd-looking parcel,
some jokes, anxiety and a final revelation.
Imagine this box, which should not be too big,
then take it and hide it with as little fuss as you can
somewhere you know its contents will be safe.

The Sea

'The tongue tells riddles:
it is as slippery as a fish.
The mind muddles things:
it is as deep as the sea.'

We did not go often to the sea. Our few journeys
to the coastal towns were an awkward business.
Where the sea itself was concerned, we were divided.
I was stirred by it to a vague romantic ecstasy, while you
found it an ideal pretext for your bitter Lichtenbergian jokes.
So when I admired the gusto of the fishing smacks,
the gulls' volplaning and the little waves
that came tilting over themselves like ostrich feathers,
you expressed your horror at what you called
'that vast untidiness – like being told someone else's dreams,
or shown a rough draft of the world's most boring epic'.
Our walks on the beach were always perfunctory, ending
with drinks in a café and talk about town.
I think of those outings now, and one occasion in particular,
when I went looking for shells that you described
as 'schoolgirls' knick-knacks . . . maritime *bondieuserie*'.
Later I caught you stooping too, and you explained
that you were trying to find 'the most imperfect pebble –
a very different matter'. I laughed and seized your hand.
There were many questions over which we were at odds,
but none so large or complex or important as the sea.

Like a Mirror

To have possessed you
like a mirror
in which you glanced once,
pulled a face and passed on.

But wait: can mirrors
be said to have memories?
Yes, there is always behind the surface
an inordinate heaviness.

So these touches of tarnish
are an attempt to express
a little of what it remembers.
How sad!

In the Echoey Tunnel

The little girl squealing
in the echoey tunnel,

scampering and squealing
just for the thrill of it,

spanking the pathway
with her own stampede of footfalls

and squealing, squealing
to make the brickwork tingle –

how fiercely she exults
in her brand-new discovery,

the gift of the tunnel
and its echoey gloom!

And then what a cheat,
to be dragged back to daylight!

Amphibiology

Like old men frolicking in sacks
seals slither on the sea-thrashed rocks.

Why does their melancholy sport
exert such a strong pull on my heart?

I could stand here for hours on end
watching them fail to make dry land.

From time to time one gains brief purchase,
adopting the pose of a Grand Duchess.

In seconds, though, a fist of surf
rises to swipe the pretender off.

Repetitive slapstick, it has the charm
of earliest documentary film.

Stuffed statesmen and wind-up warriors
turn to salute us across the years . . .

Only, in this case, something far
more ancient seems to hang in the air.

It could be the question, whether to plump
for a great evolutionary jump

or stay put in the icy brine.
May the good Lord send them a hopeful sign!

Contretemps

One lunchtime two men got in a fight.
The first tried to land a punch, but he missed.
Next moment, a barstool tipped and crashed,
the whole pub dropped to a dead hush and a tight

little space like a night-club dance floor grew
around the two bruisers in their ungainly clinch.
It was not like the movies: there was no second punch
and no attempt at fancy throwing. All they could do

was to totter on the spot, mutually clamped, grunting
and sputtering oaths, until one tripped and down
they both fell, still grappling. Each wore a frown
as stubborn as the other's. It recalled something

I'd seen long ago in a wild-life programme about
one of those grim, antiquatedly-armoured species
for whom the sexual act, through a whim of nature's,
has been made almost impossible to carry out.

Hotels

In the first hotel
I opened my wardrobe
to an ambush from childhood:
a sweet, tugging fragrance
I couldn't name.
Shuttered windows
gave on to a blind drop
and the portamenti
of amorous cats.

∾

In the second hotel
I noted that the wallpaper,
although of a strictly
geometrical pattern,
was upside-down.
A hornet arrived
the following morning,
loose-jointed, like a gunslinger.
Then it flew away.

∾

In the third hotel
none of the corridors
ran into each other
quite where expected.
My Gideon Bible
was marked at Lamentations
by an envelope addressed
to Mrs Minnie Fireberg,
Utica, NY.

∽

In the fourth hotel
I fell asleep
about nine o'clock.
Woke five hours later.
A woman in the street
was practising her giggling.
A bottle smashed.
Dawn crawled slowly
with its traffic chorus.

∽

In the fifth hotel
the complimentary stationery
carried the most
vainglorious letterhead
I have ever seen.
Why didn't I steal some?
The plumbing shuddered
in every limb
at the twist of a single tap.

In the sixth hotel
the phone was pink
and its weight felt wrong
as I lifted the receiver.
It was no one I knew.
Advice and prohibitions
in several languages
were posted by the lightswitch
in a passepartout frame.

Tyger

Early one frost-spiked morning
I was walking north from Golden Square
    in Soho, when – quite without warning –
I saw a troop of men appear
    around a corner, dragging what seemed
to be a full-grown tiger in a cage.
    Was it something I had dreamed?
It looked authentic enough: a huge
    potential man-eater that displayed
its amber teeth in a masklike snarl,
    while at the other end its tail swayed
time-bidingly . . .
            Well,
    I stood back and let them pass –
the beast on its rope-drawn carriage
    and the men heaving with less fuss
than if it had been so much inert luggage.
    Where had they come from? Where were they bound?
The tarty boutiques and design studios
    cluttering that part of town
were all shut up; ditto, the hideous,
    tear-stained, granite-clad, sixties block
whose steps are graced, you may remember,
    by a sign saying, 'WILLIAM BLAKE
WAS BORN ON 28 NOVEMBER
    1757
IN A HOUSE WHICH STOOD ON THIS SITE.'

So was it reality or vision?
Or just a trick of the morning light?

Consulting the Oracle

An old, slow and sometimes forgetful lift
takes you up to her flat on the eighth floor.
You carry in your hand some trivial gift,
ready to thrust at her inside the door.

It is accepted and then promptly hidden
in the kitchen, where you have never been.
You'd like to peep, just once, but this is forbidden
by the laws of a now fixed routine.

She comes out with the tea things on a tray
and you go with her down the unlit hall
to the front room with its museumlike display
of gilt-framed studio photographs on each wall.

Conversation gets off to a limp start.
The unreliable buses. Yesterday's snow.
What the new doctor says about her heart.
An aeroplane passes disconcertingly low.

You wonder why you've bothered, until by chance
your eye lights on a china hummingbird
and instantly she understands that glance
as an appeal. The oracle is stirred.

It was one of a pair. Its precious twin
was stolen by the soldiers. All the time
her uncle stood there clutching this one in
his big fist – so! She does a little mime.

With such authenticity, she too laughs.
You know that prim frown, that tilt of the head,
from numerous dressy family photographs,
most of whose subjects are, of course, long dead.

They can be traced from one frame to another:
the plump, horse-loving cousin who was raped . . .
the argumentative great-aunt . . . the lost brother . . .
the uncle in whose Daimler she escaped . . .

But that's enough. There will be more next time.
You bite a biscuit and sip from your cup.
Chit-chat makes do until the wheezy chime
of five o'clock, whereupon you stand up.

And your departure follows a strict pattern,
with steps down the hall, coat on, and always three
kisses bringing you to the lift's black button,
which you jab more than once, jogging its memory.

Romanesque

The Lion of Adultery
comes pouncing down.

His eyes bulge menacingly;
his mane is a blaze

of little slick flame-tufts.
Under his impending paw

a woman stands
whispering, animatedly,

words of love
into an office telephone.

෴

You see a lawn
in Arcadia,
or Suburbia.

Dapper, bearded,
two Centaurs lift
nimble forelegs to drum
the earth's taut tum.

With blithe smiles,
they represent
the innocence of the world
on a Bank Holiday Monday.

~

By the moon and padlock
it must be night
and a dangerous part of town.

One of the Unnamed Martyrs
hurries home
while, out of sight,

three club-clutching bugaboos
lie doggo.

They are King Yobbo
and his frenzied entourage.

~

A sort of Dandy Dinmont,
head cocked,
spouts like an orator.

This is the Miracle
(locally attested)
of the Dog that Spoke.

Out of the blue
he gave utterance
to all manner of mysteries.

The stars, medicine
and Holy Writ
were among the subjects he covered.

And what he said
his mistress jotted down
on the backs of old, torn envelopes.

∽

The story here
remains obscure,
but the man and woman
who stand in the mouth
of the great, gaping fish –
horned and dragonish –
and peer over its teeth
as from a tiny back garden,
seem less afraid
than might have been expected.

∽

Saint Quotidianus,
a taxi-driver in life,
appears with his emblem –
a steering-wheel.

He is flanked by the Angels
who showed him the true path:
one carries a trumpet,
the other a scrip.

Memres of Alfred Stoker

firs
born X mas day
Yer 1885
in the same burer Waping

pa a way
Ma not
being by Trade merchent Sea man
in forn parts:
all so a precher
on Land

i sow him Latter

4 of 9
not all Livig

a hard Thing Ma sad:
mirs Pale a mid Wife
in the back room bed rom
Nor wod she got Thurgh
when a ANGEL apperd over the JESUS pichire
which i got after
it Savd my Life.

☙

so i name Gabriel
which you did not no why shod you
onlie its Secd
Alfred Gabriel Joseph Stoker
Like that.

some recked she was Ling
but she was not
the ANGEL was Trew.

He had a Gold face she sad
and his Winges Gold flammy
and his ramond of Gold stufes

and in his hand he bare a BIBLE of Gold paper
and his Vois was as the Claper of Thunder over hede
with Gold Litnigg to.

pa rejoyd when he come
and spid the mars Like Candles smut
on the bed room Cornes

Than Ma had Gerge Edie Peg so on
but no ANGEL.

꙰

Edie was kind
Gerge fot
Peg the devel Mishif
Hennr did:

when 2 i nerle did
i dont remberer

When the Docter come for Hene Harry
Peg stol the Doters hat
but she was Cott:

he being Old whit berd Like the Old King
smild angerlie
give me

Ma sad ile Tan you my girl
pa a way
and she wolop Pege after

Than pa come in he sade wer is harry
and Ma cride
he past over

and pa Lift his Ey on to HEVEN
its a Merce

            ∾

all so 2 older:

Ma sad you woned
for the ANGEL blesing
she rade the BIBLE Storres in bed

Adam Eve Nore
Mose in the baskip
Joseph my name
the buring firy firnes
and the ritig on the Wall
Like at the fish Mogres winnod.

so i ha a game
in Mas cubed

i was Norrer
in the Smells
and the flod out
and i wot to Lagh all Trebling
but i did not

Than Ma buss in and Shew me.

∾

pas a venters at Sea as folos
he got in a Tempes at the Cape of Hop
a gret Wale bang his bote at Green Land
and a man eten
pa fell to
Save by a rope
at the noth Pole he saw the Ora Bols sky liths
at Mala he Lay in fever 9 days
and Leches on his hed
in Arab the King gave a cammel Ey to swolaw

and other:

his presens we a big Mask of the Affic devel
Toy animels of Eximo
and a prete Tin box of Egit for Ma

～

when 7
pa dishage Sack
by the Capten of the Vanese
his Ship at Dar solom
fiting a niger Lasker boy
did not belve in GOD.

so pa call him a wikt Hethen
wher the niger Took a Long nife
and Cut him at the Sholder
with a Skar to see
6 ins glose rinkle
Like a skin of a Lip

and the Capt sade
no coveting on my Ship
when he give pa is papers at the dock

and pa sad Ye:
its a Sine

～

2 Yers preching
waking the Land
Streets rodes
at fares Maket days
in the pub to
GODS WORD

i went

at Epsom darbie race
pa Holed my Hand
for the Gipes
with a Thin dog
the Spake a forn Langige

on a bus Top
Told the pasegers Stand
prase the LORD
but the wod not:
Hop it sun shine

No more

i need a new pensel
difrit culer

&

the river Stech of fith
a man fell in pisend
you her the Ships woo in the fog Monings
the say a Gost of Billie Okins
Lost at Sea

pa prech the Sea men and perrosterturts
when a Spanneck chap rob him for his money
which he do not have
by Gun wof
and cut him with a bottle

Ma mend it.

and Ade gone to Dulge for a Twene
i was Oldis:
Than Gerge Ede Pegge and babe Wilf

and mister Cobit a Loger of the rodes
he had a Tato on his arm
a Mer made
it Swim with a Twick.

        ∽

no Scool to bisie
Lern to read and rite the BIBLE
and drow
all so sing himms
in a good Vois with pa:

Old Cobbit do the Swize box butins
Swoll black wave Like a Sea
Edis wisel pip
in the parler

Throgh a Nith of dowt and Sorew
That
a frend in JESUS
so on

and pa sade on to us
Ye i have a Sine
to covert Scock Land
and the boy Alf to come to
for his ANGEL bidith

and Ma weep
when

To morow

∽

Scock Land

it raned

i dont rember

pa preching on a hill
with a gift of Tonges
a namile cup for monie

the Throw a cabige

      ∾

the house

fers the paler with the moggne Chairs
moslie Shut
ixep Sun day vosens:
you Smell the Old brikes Thur the florry paper

done 3 steps
to the kichin
black rage
Tin pots on hooks
the Table rub with viniker

prive at Side:

up Stares
2 beds in frowt

Mas rom pas
a big Cream Yewrer on a Thing
Like a goos

Chimmney

the crikie part you Stan wigling
wer the flor bodes Loos

Cobert in Loft

     ∽

so Gerge do my nose fitnig
Like you see
all mose Swock flat
jeles of the ANGEL
wich it Yews to be Strait
Like that:

but i drone a pichire of the same ANGEL
on a box
not Gold blake
blak wings black Skie:
wher Gerge rune at
with a devel in his Ey
and hid hit

blud gug evire were

Took to Mas bed
the wormis place
ider done hill
Slep Ther:

     ∽

i drow the Stores not now to Old
Danile and the King
the pote him in a Lions den gar gar
but the Liked his ear
Jone swolod by a Wale
to do as Told
Jebels the wikid Queen
on a Towr
the Thor her done
you get a wosie feel in the bodie
Like on a Swing
and Laseres of the ded
all so Tom Tips boy Sailer
run to Sea
whir the pirets Cote him in a baril
but he wole not Show the Tregers no not he
but Thats difret.

∾

That it yews to be
the got it all rong

being a Old ugel gisser with a chines perano
wich you Tern a hand
it jigle a Song

it was not a munnkie
it was a blow parot

∾

Alf me and Groge in own bed
Edie Pege other
Wilf in box
2 dreams.

firs i saw the devel SATAN
him Self:
with a Spike face
Alf he sade
Alf
i Try
onlie a Small pip of er

to week

it hapend a gane

Thes pesil is no good
wobley

~

its all rite
pece full
ixep the Tee vie
rubige

100 Yers

the done no

~

wher Edie Tech to fly
its esie
Like Thes
She holed my hand and junt:

at Old Sters
so we go crox the river
Like a ANGEL
no flaping

its a mirigle
ha ha:
but the men in the botes
Tell to get done

the Try to Stop us
by a foot
with a Long Stike and a hook
Like at the haber dagers you no

Edie smiles
its nice
Sun day close
Hand worm:

~

Than on day pa sad Ye:
i had a Sine
to go on to the Land of Mogro
and prech the pepil Ther
That did evel in the Sith of the LORD
Alf to come to my son
for the himms

but Ma wep saing no
he is but 9
and Little
so pa go on his owen

That we do not see a gen:
onie in a dream some Time
woking for the Land of Moggro
crox the Wold
up to Lund Waping
owr Street
at the frot door
up Stares
in the bed room
at the bed

a hoy Alf.

❧

moslie for got
to tired
its the pils

Onel some Ties memres
Like you get a wift gravie
for the kichins
in the Monig
10 a clock
it fanick ater

its winter
rember
Jake frost
Snow dirtie
and the river dirtie chugs of ice
ikles on the rops dirte to
and Ma get a coff
Like a kie in a door woned open:

a Lady mises Bussen ded
Stut to a door Step
frosen
and the Skin her face tore of
when the Lift her

Cobet gone
the peles feck him

Ma Took the Swize box to a man of Wite Chaple
2 bob
its a fare price:
and we woke to a fortine Teller
That no the Tea Lees in a yelow cup

i see a Long jirne
what
a serprise

༈

so Ma did
flow to HEVAN
being a Long jirnie
wich the forten Teller Told

a blaket on
and her Hair Lose untidie
Like a BIBLE pirson
and her face Cold.

༈

i got the pichire
SWEET JESES

༈

the Took us a way
wher i been sence:
in the ofinick firs
Than other

Edie Peg mary
Gerge run to wore
kill by a bom
and Wilf a cabin stewer
on the begum Queen

Send a Letter.

JESUS in dror:
i never see the ANGEL
onlie i no its Trow gospil
which it means i wone die
Like a sun clowid over all glomy
its in the Sky.

Fetish

I have in my possession
an angel's wingbone:
valueless, I gather,
without the certificate
of authentication
which can only be signed by a bishop.

I treasure it, however,
and almost religiously love
the sweet feel of its curve
between thumb and forefinger
deep in my jacket pocket,
the way I'm fondling it now.

From Information Received

In the small crowd
gathered to watch
the mountebank's scandalous
last performance,
there were, I understand,
two people –
a man and a woman –
whose faith in him,
far from being shattered,
was roundly confirmed.

Detaching themselves
from the crowd's sullen
and self-righteous rhubarb
of disappointment,
they left that dusty
place and took
to the highways and byways,
there to proclaim
the 'good news',
as they insist on describing it.

For, in their opinion,
a miracle did happen:
the fellow did fly,
just as he had said he would,
rapturously rocketing

to some point in the sky
of incalculable altitude,
before seeming
to change his mind
and plunging back earthwards.

To illustrate
their abstruse message,
they have some bit
of business with a stone,
or any handy object,
which they toss in the air,
telling you to fix
your mind on the moment
when it stops and allows
itself to fall.

I don't believe
we need fear this cult,
one among so many
and lacking as it does
either clear moral precepts
or potent symbolism –
some ingenious gimmick
like, say, the cross.
But the usual precautions
might still be in order.

Stones and Bones

Second Genesis

'inde genus durum sumus'
OVID, *Metamorphoses*, Book 1

Two survived the flood.
We are not of their blood,
springing instead from the bones
of the Great Mother – stones,
what have you, rocks, boulders –
hurled over their shoulders
by that pious pair
and becoming people, where
and as they hit the ground.
Since when, we have always found
something hard, ungracious,
obdurate in our natures,
a strain of the very earth
that gave us our abrupt birth;
but a pang, too, at the back
of the mind: a loss . . . a lack . . .

Skull Garden

Ewen Henderson's

For a brief while, you must stand
in this dour patch of land
and draw a deep breath.
Fragrance of life, death
and something more: the sense
of a dark intelligence
determined to conjure the whole
from a pitiless rigmarole
of making and unmaking.
To feel, within you, waking
the same idea that powers
the occasional, upstart flowers
or drives that twisted tree
through its slow dance is easy.
But what ancient seed was sown
to yield this crop of stone?
And why all these skulls blooming?
To know that would be something.

By the By

Through a helpful warder,
I soon met the legendary
Dr Spillaine,
author of the *Contradictionary* –
that vast rebuttal
of all established
lexicographical lore.
There was hardly a word
whose accepted meaning
he had not contested
and the whole enterprise rested
on his glorious disdain
for so-called alphabetical order.

Nature

The gory morsels
television brings
and deposits at our feet,
as the cat her offerings
of punctured mouse,
dishevelled-feathered bird,
leave us too often lost
for the right word.
And so we sit in silence
while across our screen,
through snowdrift and commentary,
gaunt wolverine
go loping in pursuit
of some ill-starred beast
to pluck from its scampering companions;
and the inevitable feast,
with its ripping and ravening,
is noted by
the ubiquitous camera's
unsparing eye
so matter-of-factly,
and with such a sense
of our being implicated in this,
that no pretence
of horror or detachment
will ever make do
for the lack of a spontaneous
phrase or two
by which to name and greet
the harsh event
and accommodate it between us –
as nature surely meant.

Scenes from Kafka's Marriage

1

A workman came to mend a cupboard door
that would not shut. My wife had got his name
out of the Yellow Pages. He did the job
in next to no time, and then, glancing around,
asked if there was anything else he could fix
while he was at it. To be agreeable,
we instantly drummed up a few bits and pieces:
a jittery window-frame, some plastering
and a power-point we hadn't cared to touch
for years. When I took out my wallet to pay him,
he still would not go; in fact, he's here now.
He wanders about the house, just tinkering,
drinks endless mugs of strong, sugary tea
and fills the bathroom with repellent smells.
At night we can't sleep for the noise he makes,
obsessive and rodentlike, with bradawl and screwdriver.

2

I have asked my wife not to argue with me
in public, but I don't think she understands.
This is what I most hate other couples doing:
flaring up at candlelit tables in restaurants,
or grimly bickering in supermarket aisles,
impervious to the flow of loaded trolleys.
To cope with the problem, I have devised a face
which can be switched on at a moment's notice

to cover any possible social shame.
I have practised it for weeks in front of the mirror,
so that, if my wife threatens to embarrass me,
all I shall need to do is to brandish this look,
which is somehow both merry and wise, grave and debonair,
and the entire situation will be explained.

3

The theme of last night's dream was infidelity,
although it involved not much more than an episode
of badinage and hand-squeezing with a girl
I had never met before, but whose piquant, freckled
plainness made me feel especially tender.
When I woke up, I wanted the feeling to last
and so I told my wife just what had happened,
only putting her in this strange girl's place.
It was a bad mistake. She grew suspicious
and I at once started to ornament my narrative
with ever more spurious and irrelevant details,
either invented or borrowed from other dreams.
Of course, this served to make things far worse.
It seems unfair, not being able to turn
one's involuntary flights of fancy to domestic advantage.

Feathers

After the big fire
at the feather factory,
the whole city
fell under a thick
cloud of feathers.
The boisterous guffaw
of the conflagration
had boosted them skywards,
and there they hung –
a gentle, indecisive blizzard –
for most of a week.
Just to step out of doors
was to hazard
feathers in your hair,
in your eyes, up your nostrils,
on the blade of your tongue.
Pollution or sacrament?
The cleverest minds of the day
applied themselves,
and a hundred quibbling
tracts and sermons
were written and distributed.
The incorporeality
and feathers together
to some suggested
angels, exaltation,
a new order;
to others, anarchy, death . . .
Then it began to clear.
But even when that turmoil

had subsided,
the last of the feathers
trodden into a mush
like old snow,
for a while at least
some something in the air
continued to dangle and vex us.

Fly

A fat fly fuddles for an exit
at the window-pane.
Bluntly, stubbornly, it inspects it,
like a brain
nonplussed by a seemingly simple sentence
in a book,
which the glaze of unduly protracted acquaintance
has turned to gobbledygook.

A few inches above where the fly fizzes
a gap of air
waits, but this has
not yet been vouchsafed to the fly.
Only retreat and a loop or swoop of despair
will give it the sky.

Cycle

As she proffered
that enormous gin and tonic,
the clink of ice-cubes jostling
brought to mind
an amphitheatre
scooped from a sun-lulled hillside,
where a small breeze carried
the scent of lemon-trees
and distant jostle of goat-bells,
bringing to mind
an enormous gin and tonic.

Insofar

Put on this earth to sleep,
but with no true calling for the deep

problems of utter forgetfulness
or the lurid and scary mess

of my dreams, I have deemed it wise,
insofar as I can, to specialise

in those moments on the brink
when the brain is too tired to think

but moves, still, to a chant, or thud,
that could be the song of my blood,

or some rhythm borrowed from the prose
of a book dropped as eyes close,

and I pass, alertly swooning,
into a sort of pebble-beach communing

with the great blur of the sea:
a modulation almost visionary,

like finding myself in a land
whose language I do not understand

but from which I could bring back
some wisdom, some purloined knack,

just so long as I keep
it safe from the snatches, the deep

inveiglements of sleep.

One for the Footnotes

Born in Hong Kong in 1949,
Christopher Reid was soon observed to shine
in the fields of nappy-wetting and ululation.
The leading baby of his generation,
he founded what became known as the Infantile School,
whose principle tenet, scorn for every rule,
led to a brief literary Pentecost.
Sadly, his early efforts are now lost,
as is his output from the next two years
of experimentation with bawling, tantrums, tears
and other non-verbal forms of expression. The lure
of words, however, distracted him from this pure
line of enquiry, and one can only regret
his falling under the spell of the alphabet,
which led to such work of his as survives: obscene
botches, travesties of what might have been.

The Thing and the Book

I wrote a thing in a book
which some people did not like,
and so they decided to kill me.
Now I have gone into hiding,
though I cannot escape my fear.
Shall I ever be free again?

Let me say it again:
I wrote a thing in a book
and now I must live in fear.
What will it be like,
to spend my entire life hiding?
Would it have been kinder to kill me?

They certainly wanted to kill me,
to kill me again and again.
But now I am in hiding,
so instead they must kill my book –
not the same thing, but something like –
and make the most of my fear.

Possibly they hope the fear
will be enough to kill me.
This is what they would like,
before I can do it again:
write some other book
deserving of a good hiding.

You might suppose they were hiding
their own, bigger fear –
fear of the power of a book –
in all this effort to kill me.
It won't be much of a gain,
but think that, if you like.

I don't believe that's what it's like.
I hope we're not on a hiding
to nothing, but time and again
I return to my deepest fear
that, even if they fail to kill me
and do not destroy my book,

no book so feared or disliked
will ever again find a hiding-place.
So they might as well kill us all.

Two Dogs on a Pub Roof

There are two dogs on a pub roof.
One's called Garth, the other Rolf.
Both are loud – but don't think they're all mouth.
I've been watching them and it's my belief
that they've been posted there, not quite on earth,
as emissaries of some higher truth
it's our job to get to the bottom of,
if only we can sort out the pith from the guff.
Garth's bark's no ordinary *woof, woof*:
it's a full-throttle affair, like whooping-cough,
a racking hack that shakes him from scruff
to tail in hour-long binges of holding forth
on all manner of obsessive stuff,
from pigeons and planes to not getting enough
to eat and so being ready to bite your head off.
He's whipped up in a perpetual froth
of indignation on his own behalf.
Poof! Oaf! Dwarf! Filth!
These and suchlike are among his chief
forms of salutation – and he means you, guv!
His whole philosophy, his pennyworth,
is 'All's enemy that's not self'
(with the provisional exception of his brother Rolf).
It's no joke and you don't feel inclined to laugh.
Rolf's even more frightening: his *arf! arf!*
seems designed to tear the sky in half,
every utterance an ultimate expletive,
every one a barbed shaft
aimed accurately at your midriff
and transfixing you with impotent wrath.

You and him. It bothers you both.
The thing's reciprocal, a north-south
axis that skewers the two of you like love.
You're David and Goliath, Peter and the Wolf,
Robin Hood and his Sheriff, Mutt and Jeff –
any ding-donging duo from history or myth
that's come to stand as a hieroglyph
for eternal foedom, non-stop strife,
the old Manichean fisticuffs
without which there'd be no story, no life,
and the whole cycle of birth, breath,
scoff, boff, graft, grief and death
would amount to so much waste of puff.
You're spiritual partners, hand in glove,
you and Rolfie, you and Garth,
you and the two of them up on that roof,
barking and hopping, acting tough,
flinging their taunts across the gulf
of the entire neighbourhood: *You lot down beneath!*
You got a diabolical nerve!
Who gave you permission to breathe?
This is our gaff! This is our turf!
Don't even think of crossing our path,
if you happen to value what remains of your health!
One false move and we'll show you teeth . . .
And so on. Of course, that's only a rough
translation, but it will more or less serve,
being at least the gist of the riff
that bores you mad and drives you stiff
all day long. Night, too. Nights, they work shifts.

One sleeps, while the other faces the brave
task of keeping the moon at a safe
distance and making sure the stars behave.
Which is why there are two of them. If
you've begun to wonder. As you no doubt have.
Then sometimes they'll mount an all-night rave,
Garth dancing with Rolf, Rolf with Garth –
though there's nothing queer about these two psychopaths –
and you're the inevitable wallflower, on the shelf,
surplus to requirements. Only you can't stay aloof.
Like it or lump it, you're stuck in their groove.
The joint's jumping in every joist and lath
and nobody, but nobody, is going to leave.
You're as free an agent as the flame-fazed moth
that's in thrall, flamboyantly befuddled, and not fireproof.
You're party to the party, however loth.
You belong along. You're kin. You're kith.
You're living testimony to the preposition 'with'.
You're baby, bathwater and bath.
So don't dash out with that Kalishnikov
and hope to cut a definitive swathe
through the opposition. Don't throw that Molotov
cocktail. Put down that Swiss Army knife.
Stop spitting. Stop sputtering. Don't fluster. Don't faff.
And don't be so daft, naff, duff or uncouth
as to think you're calling anyone's bluff –
let alone that of the powers above –
by threatening to depart in a huff.
They are your world, where you live,
and this is what their telegraph

of yaps and yelps, their salvoes of snuff-
sneezes, their one-note arias, oath-
fests and dog-demagoguery, their throes of gruff
throat-flexing and guffaws without mirth
are meant to signify. And it's all for your behoof!
So thanks be to Garth, and thanks to Rolf –
those two soothsayers with their one sooth,
pontificating on that pub roof –
and thanks to the God who created them both
for your enlightenment and as proof of His ruth!

While

for Lucinda

While you were confined to the gloom
of our hushed and shuttered room,
I stepped out into the sun.
Olive-trees all the way down
to the hidden, then sudden valley,
where I hoped to see things more clearly:
each tree with unique, twisted grace
asserting rights in that harsh place,
hugging its shade to itself
while flaunting an enigmatic wealth
of drab, yet glittering foliage,
under which – and this was the knowledge
I'd come for – it formed its fruit
from a pressure like unspoken thought.

Palace Floor

for Seamus Heaney

The calculations and accidents of the kiln
that gave such depth and difference to the tesserae,
their earth and flesh tones, unanalysably tertiary,
by which the breasts and pot-belly of the Sea Goddess
were made so round and real that he was scared to caress them,
drew him again and again to inspect that chamber,
and even when forced abroad he would seem to hear her,
from her company of octopus and swordfish, calling, calling.

The Sirens

after Homer and for Christopher Logue

As I was putting my men in the picture,
a fair wind brought us abreast
of the Sirens' island, then dropped.
Dead calm. Waves spellbound.
But the crew leapt straight up, furled the sail
and stowed it, then back at their oars
whipped the water till it blazed white.
I took a slab of wax, chopped it,
kneaded it, and soon, with the sun's help,
it was soft enough to stop the ears
of my shipmates. And they in turn
stood me against the mast and lashed me
tightly to it. Then back to their oars again.
Just as we came within hailing distance,
the Sirens, catching sight of our progress,
sent out this eerily voluptuous song:
> *Draw near, Odysseus, pride of the Achaians,*
> *lay to awhile and listen to our voices.*
> *No one has ever yet sailed past this island*
> *without hearing the music of our sweet lips*
> *or going on his way a wiser man.*
> *We know what was suffered on the plains of Troy*
> *by Argives and Trojans, at the whim of the gods.*
> *We know all that happens on this bountiful earth.*
That's what they sang. I wanted to hear more,
so I yelled at my shipmates and shook my frenzied head at them,
but they leant to their oars and pulled and pulled,
while Perimedes and Eurylochos
jumped up, found some extra rope

and tied me even tighter.
Once we'd left the Sirens behind us
and were out of range of their outlandish voices,
my men removed the wax from their ears
and freed me from my own confinement.

Smoking and Drinking

A Pipe

after Baudelaire

I am a poet's pipe.
Cursory inspection
of my African complexion
will tell you he's the hard-smoking type.

When things are really bad,
I send up puffs as steady
as from some cottage where supper's ready
for the homecoming farm lad.

To keep his soul calm,
I can make a swaying hammock unroll
in blue wisps from my fiery bowl

and spread a potent balm,
soothing to his heart and kind
to his exhausted mind.

At the Green Man

after Rimbaud

For a week now, I'd been blistering my feet
on the stony country roads. Then I came to Hemel Hempstead.
At the Green Man, I asked for some French bread,
butter, and ham with still a hint of its oven heat.

Contentedly stretching my legs under the green-topped table,
I'm studying the décor, when – wa-hey! up flies
the bar-girl with her voluminous tits and flashing eyes.
(Getting past those defences shouldn't prove much trouble.)

She smiles as she hands me a big Staffordshire dish
of bread already buttered and home-baked ham,
all pink and white and keen to salute everyone
with garlicky bonhomie. Plus, there's a bottle to replenish
my long glass, which instantly heaves up oodles of foam
in its haste to be blessed by a last-minute ray of the sun.

Cigar Smoke

after Mallarmé

The whole soul summed up
as we breathe it out
in a few leisurely puffs
that dissolve in the general cloud

attests to a cigar
burning capably
so long as its bright fire
kisses the ash goodbye

likewise should your lips
give wing to some sentimental song
be sure to omit
anything real or debasing

too clear a sense destroys
literature's mysteries.

Memoirs of a Publisher

after Li Po

Such a good lunch
suddenly it's evening

stains on the tablecloth
I totter outside

where have the pigeons gone?
where are the taxis?

A City that Marco Polo Missed

for Sara Fanelli

Whatever the nature of your journey, whether you've been tossed
this way and that on the blustery epic of the Atlantic Ocean,
thwarted by the tangled syntax of the Brazilian jungle, or lost
somewhere in the interminable theological treatise of the Sahara,
there is no more pleasant emotion
than to find yourself suddenly at the gates of the city of Sara.

Because it is always on the move, its precise extent is a mystery;
but the traveller who takes it in slowly, as it were a page at
    a time,
will learn something of its peculiar customs and history
and soon feel at home. Street manners are elaborately good;
there are skyscrapers, but no crime;
both birds and insects wear hats; the entire populace loves
    picnic food.

Arrows, asterisks and exclamation-marks are a major feature
of the local dialect, and musical notation hangs like fruit in
    the air.
You may occasionally run into some extravagant creature
with an odd number of legs, a whirligig tail or unmatching eyes,
but there is nothing to fear
in this perfectly egalitarian state, no one to dislike or despise.

People say that the architect and the law-giver of the city
were one and the same. Indeed, some believe it was a child,
who took a sheet of grown-up graphpaper and filled it up
     with witty
frisks and twiddles, which then sprang to a life of their own.
This is a place that encourages wild
fabulations, but where no dog is without its necessary bone.

Thirty-three Paroxysms

for Kay Henderson and in memory of Ewen

He talked like a pessimist and acted like an optimist.

His despair of humanity was one of humanity's best reasons for hope.

He spoke eloquently against the danger of words.

His hand gestures showed that for him ideas were tactile.

His jokes were profoundly silly.

Puns, spoonerisms and other verbal games were among his preferred oracular devices.

He had a nose for the essential – a broken nose.

He entrusted his weightiest statements to a fragile medium.

In his art, the creative and the destructive possibilities of fire were one and the same thing.

His pots were built as monuments to impermanence.

They have the repose of volcanoes.

They aspire to the condition of questions, not answers.

Most of his vessels leak.

Whether his bowls and dishes contain fruit or stand empty, they suggest cornucopias.

While his paintings explore three dimensions, his sculptural work meditates on four.

He pursued a vision of wholeness by means of collage.

His drawings do not confuse grace with gracefulness.

Prettiness, elegance, refinement and symmetry were all traps he took care to avoid.

His garden used a time-honoured English decorative art form to express new and outlandish truths.

Birds, frogs, slugs and insects know his work better than many art experts.

He despised most critics for betraying their art.

Music was his ideal form of sculpture.

Machaut, Gesualdo, Bach, Berlioz, Stravinsky and Ligeti were all his exact contemporaries.

He was a Modernist, of the school of Lascaux.

He believed in the eternal youth of the ancient world.

Nature was his culture.

Like any great teacher, he wanted us to teach ourselves.

His cat and his dog were his most attentive students, and he was theirs.

His anger sprang from generosity.

He was a gentle man whom the powerful found fierce.

He had great appetites but little greed.

Because he loved life, he accepted death.

Now that he is gone, we look for him everywhere.

A Scarecrow's Theory of Art

for Rob Woolner

Two eyes, peeled,
step into a field
of coloured mud.
The field is a flood
of marks and matter.
The field is a scatter
of planes and lines,
a system of signs
bounded by what
the field is not.
The field is a figment
of mind and pigment,
of hand and weather
working together
in conflict and discourse.
The field is a force.
The field is a field
where two eyes, peeled
to appraise the new
and eternal view
that the painter has made
from shape and shade,
feel the light
stiffen and bite
like a brisk gust
from nowhere, then must
begin gleaning
their own meaning.

The Phone-Fox

for Jane Feaver

We were talking about Ted Hughes,
    when the corner of my eye
twitched to the fact of a fox
    on the flat, tar-papered roof
of the chapel-of-rest next door.
What a moment to choose!
I watched as it spelt itself out
    from shadows of the far-side garden
into clear sunlight,
    at which point I gave a shout
which must have sounded crazy.
Then it trotted about,
inspecting different views.
And then it did a quick jig
once around itself,
    lay down, extended its forepaws
and cocked its muzzle for a big,
    tasty, air-licking yawn.
Unbiddable, unbidden,
    this was a genuine fox
of the Inner London variety,
    now enjoying its own society
on top of the squat brick box
    where they bring the newly dead.
Accident or sign,
    I was sorry nothing I said
could make it real for you
    at your end of the line.

Bollockshire

You've zoomed through it often enough
on the long grind north, the grim dash south –
    why not take a break?
    Slip off the motorway
at any one of ten tangled junctions
and poke your nose, without compunction,
    into the unknown.
    Get systematically lost.
At the first absence of a signpost,
opt for the least promising lane,
    or cut into the truck traffic
    along some plain,
perimeter-fence-lined stretch of blacktop
heading nowhere obvious.
    Open your mind
    to the jarring yellow
of that hillside rape crop, the grim Norse green
of that fir plantation, where every tree
    steps forward to greet you
    with the same zombie gesture
of exclamation, the last-ditch brown of –
what could it be? Something to do with pigs?
    Row on row
    of miniature Nissen huts
laid out like a new speculative estate
in acres of glistening mud, behind an electronic gate . . .
    But don't stop now.
    Press on,
undistracted by the lush hedgerows
(of which there are none)

or the silence of the songbirds.
    Other counties
can match these. It's the essence of Bollockshire
you're after: its secrets, its blessings and bounties.
        So keep driving,
            past sly-windowed farms,
lying there with hoards of costly machinery
in their arms, like toys they won't share;
            past Bald Oak Hill,
                down the more shaded side of which
the Bollockshire Hunt has scuffled
many a morning to its kill;
            past St Boldric's church,
                with the slant steeple,
which Cromwell's lads once briefly visited,
leaving behind them saints re-martyred,
            the Virgin without her head;
            past Bewlake Manor's
dinky Gothic gatehouse, now the weekend habitat
of London media or money people;
            past the isolated
            Bulldog pub,
with its choice of scrumpies, microwave grub,
bouncy castle and back-room badger fights –
            past all that,
                until, if you are lucky,
you hit the famous ring road. Thrown down
decades ago, like a gigantic concrete garland
            around the county town,
                riddled and plugged

by the random dentistry of maintenance work
and chock-a-block with contraflow,
    it must, you feel,
    be visible from the moon.
One road sign hides another. There are orange cones
galore. Each cultivated roundabout island
    is, if possible, more off-key
    than the one before.
But don't stick here all afternoon:
Blokeston itself has to be seen,
    via the brick maze
    of its by-gone industrial outskirts.
This is where Silas Balk invented his machine
for putting a true, tight twist in string,
    where they once supplied the world
    with all it needed
of bicycle saddles and cigarette papers,
where cough syrup was king.
    Round the corner,
    just when you least expect,
there's Blokeston FC, home of 'The Blockers',
and Blokeston Prison, by the same no-frills architect.
    Unmissable from any position,
    the Bulwark Brewery
stands up in a haze of its own malty vapours,
which even today's counterwafts of Tandoori
    cannot contest.
    Now, turn east or west,
and you'll find yourself on a traffic planner's
one-way inward spiral, passing at speed

through older and older
parts of town –
the impeccable Georgian manners
of Beauclerc Square, built on slave-trade money;
bad Bishop Bloggs's school;
the crossroads where
the Billhook Martyrs were tortured and burned –
until you reach the river Bleak.
Squeeze, if you can,
over the Black Bridge,
then park and pay – assuming this isn't the week
of the Billycock Fair, or Boiled Egg Day,
when they elect the Town Fool.
From here, it's a short step
to the Bailiwick Hall Museum and Arts Centre.
As you enter, ignore the display
of tankards and manacles, the pickled head
of England's Wisest Woman;
ask, instead, for the Bloke Stone.
Surprisingly small, round, featureless,
pumice-grey,
there it sits, dimly lit,
behind toughened glass, in a room of its own.
Be sure to see it, if you've a taste
for this sort of primitive conundrum.
Most visitors pass
and won't even leave their vehicles,
keen by this time to make haste
back to the life they know,
and to put more motorway under them.

North London Sonnet

for Lucinda

A boom-box blats by,
less music than sonic muscle
assaulting the night sky,
a pumped-up hustle-bustle

which manages to disturb
the twirly, needling alarm
of a car tucked into the kerb –
its mantra, or charm –

but that, too, soon quiets
and you sleep on, proof
against the rumpuses and riots
encircling our roof,

till my switching off the light
prompts a muffled *Good night.*

The Myth of the Mouth

Before all this scribble
before all this babble
before even the first word
there was the Mouth

Silent and solitary
yawn-shaped and endlessly empty
it filled the universe
in which it lived

But every being
even the first one
requires an other
to confirm that it exists

So the Mouth tried
to give birth to another Mouth
its mightiest efforts
producing just words

More and more words
the harder it tried
proliferating and spilling
through the available space of the universe
till the Mouth their parent
was squeezed out forever

Now the words
have found other lesser mouths
poor simulacra
of the original enunciator
to occupy
for their own short lives

Their incessant multiplication
is driven by a yearning
for the Mouth they have lost

Oracle

He found the oracle
in a hole in the ground

No not exactly
the oracle was
the hole itself
made by workmen
gouged from compacted
city road subsoil
with picks and power tools
then left to gape
showing enquirers
its strata of tarmac
cobblestones hard core
and stiff yellow clay
nothing more

When Mr Mouth
asked it his question
it thought for a moment
before uttering
a single syllable
of which the vowel
was lighter than a cough
of dusty air
and consonant less
than the mineral rustle
of grit against grit

Not much you might think
but Mr Mouth
having heard what he had heard
went on his way
wiser and happier
into the changed
and changing future

Recital

Like one of those trespassing mortals who must pay
with their lives for a glimpse of forbidden divinity
Mr Mouth does not know which way to look

when the singer whose total command of her art
has held the house spellbound turns her gaze full on him
opens her throat lets loose her topmost note and the one

unavoidable thing is her tongue in its specialised ecstasy
nude lithe moist arched and vibrating
a revelation from which he can only

pray to escape with his soul

Venus Fly-Trap Dream Song

Doodling along in the form of a fly
    an innocent amiable chap
Mr Mouth arrived at a patch of the sky
    that was off the edge of the map

Though he knew he was lost he was blithe and spry
    heedless of any mishap
because every fly has a multiple eye
    to watch out for a swat or a slap

And with no nasty beastie lurking nearby
    ready to whop him or zap
out a prehensile tongue he asked himself why
    not nip down for a bit of a nap

What a fearful fate for so fine a guy
    that at that moment he should clap
his myriad eye on that none too shy
    femme fatale the Venus Fly-Trap

Which as soon as her trigger-hairs sense a fly
    close on it with a snap
like a yawn in reverse or a silent sigh
    cruelly leaving no gap

Mr Mouth awoke with an anguished cry
    and phoned his shrink in a flap
to be told his dream meant he wanted to die
    and a whole heap of other crap

The Hole in Victorian Literature

The rabbit-hole
down which Alice fell
is a classic symbol
    begins Professor Mouth

The lecture hall
is hushed as a bell
waiting to be tolled
    so he continues

But not sexual
stunning them all
with this dismissal
    of a Freudian commonplace

They are utterly baffled
what other hole
could Lewis Carroll
    have had in mind

A pause then *Oral*
he adds with a smile
as if he had pulled
    a live rabbit from a top-hat

Well well well
another old fool
with his whimsical drivel
    as they might have guessed

There's the clatter-dance of a pencil
general shuffle
and someone tries to stifle
    an expanding yawn

The Rev Mr Mouth's Controversial Sermon

His text was taken
from the apocryphal
Acts of St Thomas
his favourite disciple

the passage where
not satisfied
with a mere glimpse
of the gash in Christ's side

having gauchely asked
permission to touch it
Thomas puts his finger
to the lips of the wound

as if to hush it

Adam and Eve

What more tragic picture
than the one Mr Mouth
is staring at now

Two naked figures
expelled forever
from the garden of their happiness

Tormented postures
hands trying to hide
his eyes her private parts

And that terrifying aperture
the fathomless blackness
of her howl

Against his own nature
Mr Mouth just stands there
gaping back

Régime Change in Utopia

Unanimously elected President of Utopia
Mr Mouth steps out on to the balcony
of the fairytale presidential palace
to address the well-behaved mob below

Scarcely visible behind the usual
bouquet of microphones he waits for a lull
in the chorus of roaring before he can begin
his speech to the people and the listening world

Using Esperanto a language he has spoken
fluently since the day he was born
he announces a new national holiday
Thank you very much sir shouts the crowd

Next and somewhat more surprisingly
he declares war on neighbouring Dystopia
the far side of the mountain range dividing
Esperanto from Desperanto speakers

At once the benign police move in
to arrest a man whose untidy parting
suggests Dystopian blood and a woman
cheering in a could-be Desperanto accent

Om

What a satisfying syllable
well-round well-deep
unimprovably plain
it comes without taint
of meaning or metaphor

Sitting on a mat
in a knot of his own legs
Mr Mouth relishes
the rare pleasure
of saying it and tasting it
at the same time

Embryonic speech balloon
nothing-flavoured gobstopper
it fills him with emptiness
and puts such a blissful
gloat on his face
that his Master has gravely
started to wonder
if he'll ever get the point

Dying Words

Back in the same hospital
from which he began his journey
Mr Mouth lies
limp as a puppet
snug as a baby

A less garrulous baby
than he was then

A nurse has washed
and combed his long silver beard for him
folded his hands
in a faintly saintly arrangement

Visitors gathered
about his bed
dutifully await
some wise final pronouncement

When a dawdling cloud effaces
the late-afternoon sun
then negligently
reveals it again
in evident pain
Mr Mouth raises
a gnarled pontifical finger

And instead of speaking
points to a notice
with its simple truth

NIL BY MOUTH

Obol

With all due ceremony
    they closed his mouth
on the single coin
    tucked under his tongue
indispensable
    and non-transferrable
fare for the ferry journey
    the last he would make

Little did they know
    that before he reached
the bank of the Styx
    he would suck it to nothing
like a pastille or a peppermint
    leaving just a whiff
of bronze on his breath
    his dead man's breath
to pay for passage
    to the other side

Taking pity
    as he'd never done before
and never would again
    the ferryman accepted it

The Unfinished

I

Sparse breaths, then none –
and it was done.

Listening and hugging hard,
between mouthings
of sweet next-to-nothings
into her ear –
pillow-talk-cum-prayer –
I never heard
the precise cadence
into silence
that argued the end.
Yet I knew it had happened.

Ultimate calm.

Gingerly, as if
loth to disturb it,
I released my arm
from its stiff vigil athwart
that embattled heart
and raised and righted myself,
the better to observe it.

Kisses followed,
to mouth, cheeks, eyelids, forehead,
and a rigmarole
of unheard farewell
kept up as far
as the click of the door.

After six months, or more,
I observe it still.

2

Those last few days
of drug-drowse, coma-comfort,
friends came, if not as many
as before, to keep her company,
to talk, to weep.
At each arriving voice,
I thought I saw
a faint, fleeting
muscular effort
adjust her mouth and jaw
as if in greeting,
as if for a kiss.

But how could that have been?

I talked, too, read aloud
from her favourite Yeats,
or played the last, great
Schubert quartets –
the one in G
that, with whole-hearted
ambivalence,
weighs in the balance
the relative merits
of major and minor
and struggles to postpone the choice.

While I cultivated
my clumsy, husbandly
bedside manner,
she lay as her nurses had arranged her:
reposeful beloved,
stark stranger –
or something in between.

3

'Gently, little boat,
across the ocean float':
Auden's words,
which Stravinsky's ear
slanted, tilted, made more
liltingly awkward.
Out of the whole
ragbag repertoire
of songs she loved to sing,
this lullaby-barcarolle
might have been just the thing,
if the bed had been a boat,
and the boat going anywhere.

But, as a wise man said,
'Death is not
an event in life.'
Nor is it a journey.

The hospice bed
bearing my wife
stood in a hushed
back room, moored fast
to the physical facts
of this singular life.
Only in that space
of the mind where the wilful
metaphors thrive

has it now pushed
out into open sea
and begun to travel
beyond time and place,
never to arrive.

4

'Come on, girls,
you can do it!'

The force of the fit
that, after weeks
of merciless paralysis,
shocked her upright,
shouting mad things –
'I can see you
behind that box!' –
frightened me, of course.
Furious as I'd never
known her before
in any of our quarrels,
she was suddenly, somehow,
strong as an ox.
But I held her tight.

'Bastards! Bastards!'

Even now,
theatrical training
lent strength to her lungs
and unmistakable meaning
to this sibylline binge
of gabble, rant and swear-words.

A kindly nurse
hurried towards us
with a syringe.

5

No imp or devil
but a mere tumour
squatted on her brain.
Without personality
or ill humour,
malignant but not malign,
it set about doing –
not evil,
simply the job
tumours have always done:
establishing faulty
connections, skewing
perceptions, closing down
faculties and functions
one by one.

Hobgoblin, nor foul fiend;
nor even the jobsworth slob
with a slow, sly scheme to rob
my darling of her mind
that I imagined;
just a tumour.

Between which and the neat
gadget with the timer
that eased drugs into her vein,
she contrived to maintain
her identity

unimpaired and complete,
resolved to meet
death with all gallantry
and distinction.

6

Dead Souls enjoyed
but put aside
midway, *Sense
and Sensibility* done,
she wanted another Austen:
Northanger Abbey.
I brought it in next day.
From the runaway
long first paragraph
onwards, she was happy,
with a staring, intense
involvement and full play
of her relishing laugh
(one faculty not yet affected).

A few sessions in,
we were still in Bath
when she stopped me and said,
'You know, this is so good,
I don't understand
why it's never been written down.'
I held up the book,
reminded her how often
she'd read it before,
argued, grew annoyed,
but nothing shook
that rapt conviction.

So, at her insistence,
in my crabbed hand
I wrote out several sentences,
then some more –
just to be sure
that a great work of comic fiction
would not be forgotten.

7

A warm croissant
and cappuccino
were our morning rite:
alternate bites
of flaking, buttery pith;
then the straw guided
into her mouth
and the coffee making
its hesitant ascent
with puckered sucks
that just as stutteringly subsided.

Tougher work
than playing an oboe,
yet performed with a gusto
that customarily took
more than her fair share.
Not that I was measuring!
Rather, it was a case
of pride and delight
in such simple pleasuring:
the look on her face,
pure, animal appetite.

Therefore, not heart-breaking,
to picture her
across a table
in some quiet French seaside spot,

scanning a cluttered
plateau de fruits de mer
with its full surgical couvert,
and about to clatter
her way through the lot
as slowly as she was able.

8

By good luck, the hospice
was situated
in a foodie haven,
a North London
village-cosmopolis
of delicatessens.

Her first visitors seated,
I was instructed
to run out and find
Żubrówka and Polish
appetisers.
I came back with 'Russian'
vodka, warm,
and *antipasti*.
She seemed not to mind,
and later I got better
at fulfilling such errands
to the letter.

Food and friends,
treats and surprises:
all that she deemed necessary
assumed the tragi-
comic form
of Chekhovian picnics
at our end of the ward,
which she directed, or conducted,

with frail, airy
emphases and flourishes
of her right arm –
the one limb so far spared.

9

How bright the wit,
the circumstance-mocking
theatrical badinage, burned.
To a friend concerned
she might be tired
I heard her say,
'Exhausted people
leave the hospice all day,
and I just carry on talking.'

To another, catching
a glimpse of her own
undimmable spirit:
'I'm being radiant
again, aren't I!'

It was inspired,
brave, funny and subtle
of her to interpret
the role of patient
so flat against type –
cheering her nurses,
feeding advice and support
to friends, encouraging
her husband to address his
possible future
with something of her hope.

It's not in his nature,
but he can try.

10

When the brush had started
tugging out random
tufts and clumps
of springy brown hair
from her outgrown bob,
she asked me to shave
the whole lot off.

Fractious, half-hearted,
I took on the job,
began maladroitly,
then finished it
with a perfectionist's care.

Revealed: a handsome,
unabashed smoothness
I couldn't stop wanting
to fondle and kiss.

Wasn't it something –
that the cup of my hand
and curve of her clean scalp
should turn out to be
such an intimate fit!

The pull to palp
and pamper that round shape,
to learn its lineaments
and feel the hint

of a hint of light stubble
pushing through,
was irresistible.
Virgin landscape,
so neat and so new!

11

So like a baby,
with her bald head
and one working arm
clear of the blanket
that the ambulance men
had folded her in,
but a baby with wide, wise,
learning eyes
and an unexpected
gift of speech,
she proceeded first
to puzzle, then charm,
her attendants with a burst
of questions and comments
on everything in reach:
from the gadgets and fixtures
to the colour of her blanket,
a pragmatic scarlet;
then, as the vehicle
speeded along,
the swivelling, wrong-
way-round, receding
view through the window
of just the tops
of houses and shops,
which made a familiar
route hard to follow;
via this, that and the other,

till – how, I can't think –
they were onto the subject
of favourite drinks,
and no one objected
when she nominated
as the most delicious
of all, champagne.

A Scattering

I expect you've seen the footage: elephants,
finding the bones of one of their own kind
dropped by the wayside, picked clean by scavengers
and the sun, then untidily left there,
    decide to do something about it.

But what, exactly? They can't, of course,
reassemble the old elephant magnificence;
they can't even make a tidier heap. But they can
hook up bones with their trunks and chuck them
    this way and that way. So they do.

And their scattering has an air
of deliberate ritual, ancient and necessary.
Their great size, too, makes them the very
embodiment of grief, while the play of their trunks
    lends sprezzatura.

Elephants puzzling out
the anagram of their own anatomy,
elephants at their abstracted lamentations –
may their spirit guide me as I place
    my own sad thoughts in new, hopeful arrangements.

Late

Late home one night, I found
she was not yet home herself.
So I got into bed and waited
under my blanket mound,
until I heard her come in
and hurry upstairs.
My back was to the door.
Without turning round,
I greeted her, but my voice
made only a hollow, parched-throated
k-, k-, k- sound,
which I could not convert into words
and which, anyway, lacked
the force to carry.
Nonplussed, but not distraught,
I listened to her undress,
then sidle along the far side
of our bed and lift the covers.
Of course, I'd forgotten she'd died.
Adjusting my arm for the usual
cuddle and caress,
I felt mattress and bedboards
welcome her weight
as she rolled and settled towards me,
but, before I caught her,
it was already too late
and she'd wisped clean away.

Afterlife

As if she couldn't bear not to be busy and useful
after her death, she willed her body to medical science.

Today, as a number of times before, I walked
past the institution that took her gift, and thought,

'That's where my dead wife lives. I hope they're treating her
kindly.'

The dark brick, the depthless windows, gave nothing away,
but the place seemed preferable to either Heaven or Hell,

whose multitudes meekly receive whatever the design teams
and PR whizzes of religion have conjured up for them.

My wife is in there, somewhere, doing practical work:
her organs and tissues are educating young doctors

or helping researchers outwit the disease that outwitted her.
So it's a hallowed patch of London for me now.

But it's not a graveyard, to dawdle and remember and mope in,
and I had work to do, too, in a different part of town.